# STEM DETECTIVES

# THE CASE OF THE LOST ROBOT

WRITTEN BY
**William Anthony**

D1710494

## CRABTREE
PUBLISHING COMPANY
WWW.CRABTREEBOOKS.COM

**Author:** William Anthony

**Editorial director:** Kathy Middleton

**Design:** Amy Li

**Proofreaders:** Melissa Boyce, Janine Deschenes

**Prepress technician:** Ken Wright

**Print coordinator:** Katherine Berti

All facts, statistics, web addresses and URLs in this book were verified
as valid and accurate at time of writing.
No responsibility for any changes to external websites or references can
be accepted by either the author or publisher.

**Photo Credits:** All images courtesy of Shutterstock.
With thanks to Getty Images, Thinkstock Photo and iStockphoto.
**Cover** – Jemastock, Recurring images – Macrovector (wire background, the
STEM Detectives,), stickerama (Bob), MicroOne, tn-prints – Gaidamashchuk,
Golden Vector, MaryDesy (elements in video still on page 17 and 19).
Monash, , p2–3 – Tartila, notkoo, p4–5 – ProStockStudio, 6–7 – notkoo,
p8–9 – ProStockStudio, Macrovector, p10–11 – Crystal Eye Studio, notkoo,
p12–13 – Macrovector, p14–15 – Bibadash, Macrovector, notkoo, p16–17
– Bibadash, Macrovector, kasha malasha, p18–19 – kasha malasha, notkoo,
p20–21 – Macrovector, p22–23 – Macrovector, p24 – Tartila

**Library and Archives Canada Cataloguing in Publication**

Title: The case of the lost robot / William Anthony.
Names: Anthony, William (Children's author), author.
Description: Series statement: STEM detectives | Originally published:
  King's Lynn: BookLife, 2020.
  | Includes index.
Identifiers: Canadiana (print) 20200225464 | Canadiana (ebook)
  20200225472 | ISBN 9780778782308
  (hardcover) | ISBN 9780778782346 (softcover) | ISBN 9781427126160
  (HTML)
Subjects: LCSH: Puzzles—Juvenile literature. | LCSH: Problem solving—
  Juvenile literature. | LCGFT:
  Puzzles and games.
Classification: LCC GV1507.D4 A583 2021 | DDC j793.73—dc23

**Library of Congress Cataloging-in-Publication Data**

Available on request

## Crabtree Publishing Company

www.crabtreebooks.com     1–800–387–7650
Published by Crabtree Publishing Company in 2020

©2020 BookLife Publishing Ltd.

Printed in the U.S.A./012020/CG20200429

**Published in Canada**
**Crabtree Publishing**
616 Welland Ave.
St. Catharines, Ontario
L2M 5V6

**Published in the United States**
**Crabtree Publishing**
347 Fifth Ave
Suite 1402-145
New York, New York 10016

# BE A STEM DETECTIVE!

Welcome, new recruit! We're so happy that you want to join the STEM Detectives.

We're experts in STEM, which stands for science, technology, engineering, and

math. We use all of these subjects to help us solve mysteries at our school.

# THE TEAM

**ASHA**
Math Queen

**KIM**
Science Boss

**SANJAY**
Technology Whiz

**LUCAS**
Engineering Ace

**iGUMBO**
RoboDog Sidekick

MISSING

# THE CHALLENGE

The STEM Detectives need your help to solve their next case. When you see this symbol, the Detectives will ask you to solve a problem, carry out an experiment, or look for clues. Complete each task before you turn the page. You can check your answers on page 24.

9:00 a.m. meant the start of a new day at Stemberry School. For the STEM Detectives, it also meant the start of a new case.

iGumbo

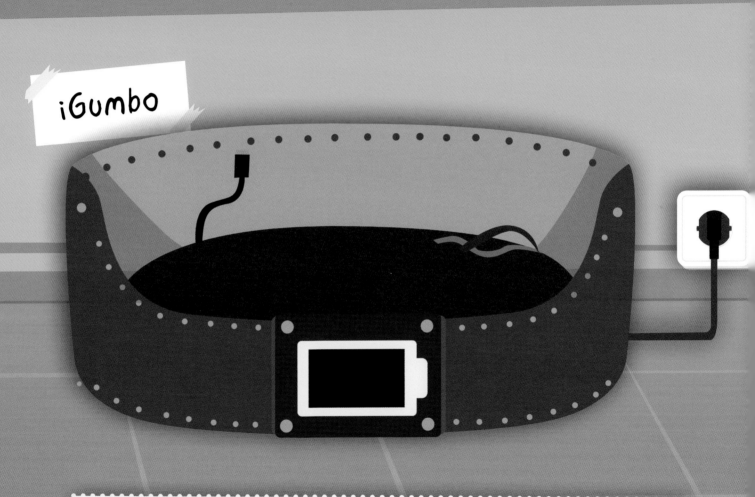

Each morning, iGumbo was waiting in his charging bed. Today, however, he was nowhere to be seen!

"Where could iGumbo be?" asked Kim.
"I have no idea," said Lucas. "Hey, Mr. Jenkins, have you seen iGumbo today?"

"I saw him in the cafeteria and on the playground this morning," replied Mr. Jenkins, the janitor.

We can track iGumbo on this electronic map of the school. One of these three lines shows iGumbo's path this morning. Which line is the one we are looking for?

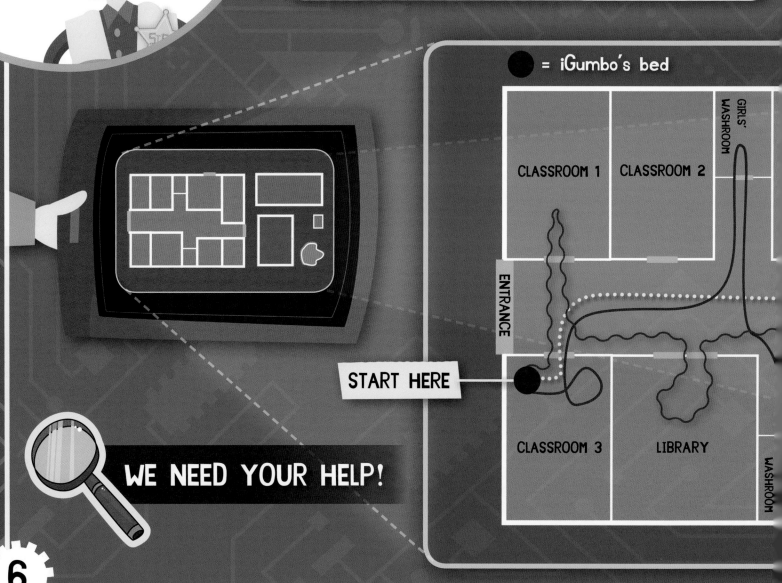

● = iGumbo's bed

GIRLS' WASHROOM

CLASSROOM 1    CLASSROOM 2

ENTRANCE

START HERE

CLASSROOM 3    LIBRARY

WASHROOM

WE NEED YOUR HELP!

Mr. Jenkins saw iGumbo in the cafeteria and the playground. That means the line that passes through both of those places will lead to iGumbo! Where does the correct line end?

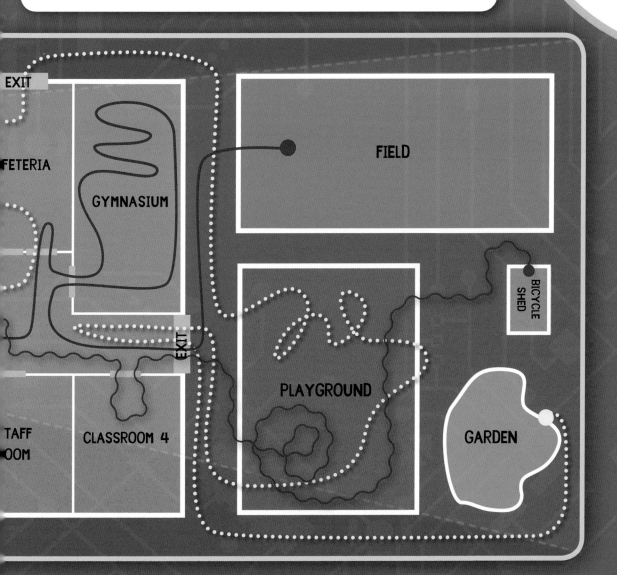

EXIT

FETERIA

GYMNASIUM

FIELD

EXIT

BICYCLE SHED

PLAYGROUND

TAFF OOM

CLASSROOM 4

GARDEN

By the garden? I think you're right.

"He's by the garden," said Lucas. "Let's go!" The Detectives ran off in search of iGumbo. When they got to the garden, they were disappointed.

8

iGumbo was still nowhere to be seen. "I don't understand. Was the tracker lying?" asked Asha.

"No, something's just wrong. Very wrong," said Lucas.

I have an idea, but I need your help. I can check iGumbo's algorithm on the tablet. An algorithm is a set of instructions that a computer follows. iGumbo's algorithm usually looks like this:

Receive task

Start task

Wait for new task

Antenna

Send location from antenna

Send location from antenna

Recharge in charging bed

Complete task

WE NEED YOUR HELP!

10

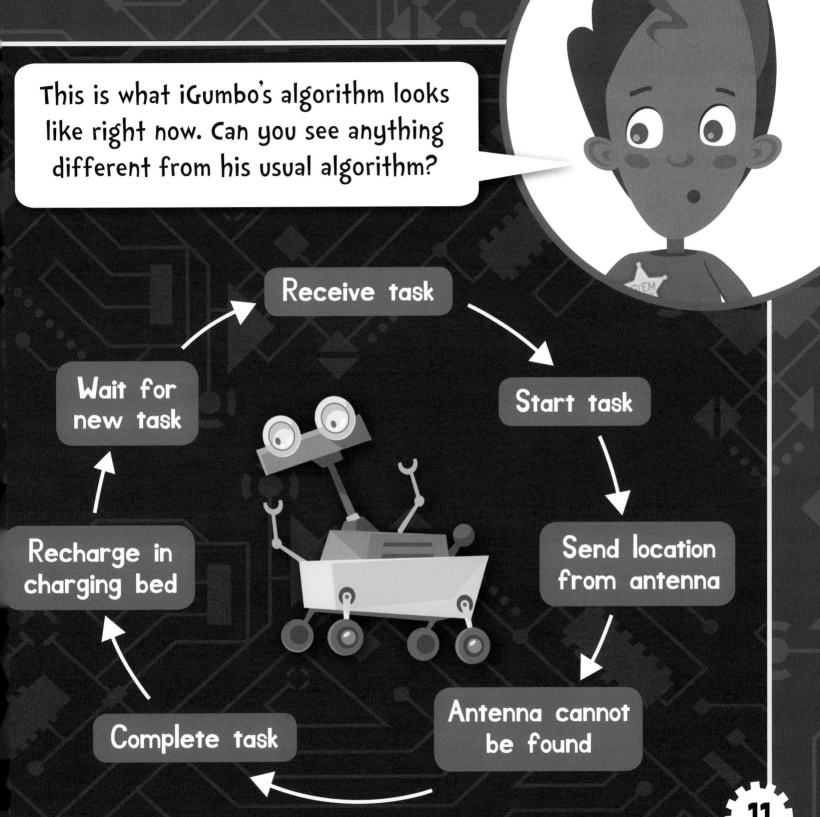

Nice work! iGumbo's antenna is missing. Without the antenna, iGumbo cannot send us his location.

"It looks like iGumbo lost his antenna. It must be around here somewhere," said Sanjay.

12

"Over here!" shouted Kim.
She had found iGumbo's antenna.
"Why is it covered in fur?" asked Asha.

"Maybe something furry stole iGumbo!
What if it was a grizzly bear?"
said Lucas nervously.

13

"Do you know when iGumbo's algorithm broke?" Asha asked Sanjay.
"About six hours ago," he said. "Let's go and see Mr. Jenkins.
He might have camera footage of what happened."
Mr. Jenkins was snoozing at his desk.

We need to ask Mr. Jenkins to rewind the camera. iGumbo lost his antenna six hours ago. It is 2:00 p.m. now. What time did iGumbo lose his antenna?

WE NEED YOUR HELP!

"Sure," said a shaky Mr. Jenkins.
"There he is!" shouted Sanjay.
"He's with a lot of animals, but
at least there's no grizzly bear,"
said Lucas. That was a relief.

Earlier, we found iGumbo's antenna tangled up in some fur. By looking closely at the fur, we can find out which animal broke iGumbo's antenna. This will lead us one step closer to finding iGumbo!

WE NEED YOUR HELP!

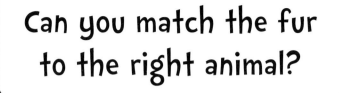

"Of course," replied Mr. Jenkins. "He's my dog! His name is Hugo. His hobbies include playing fetch, chewing shoes, and bumping into things!"

"Would Hugo steal iGumbo?" asked Sanjay. "Steal him? No way! He would just be happy to find a new friend," said Mr. Jenkins.

BANG!

"Well, where could they be?" wondered Kim. Suddenly, there was a loud BANG!

22

The door burst open. Hugo stumbled in with a bucket on his head. He was followed by iGumbo! It seems that even robot dogs can be clumsy too.

# WELL DONE!

You helped us solve the case! We couldn't have done it without your super skills in science, technology, engineering, and math. You have earned the right to wear a STEM Detectives badge!

Scan this QR code and print off your badge. We'll see you when it is time for our next case!

# ANSWERS

### PAGE 7
The correct line is yellow. It ends at the garden.

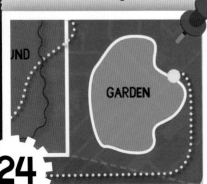

### PAGE 11

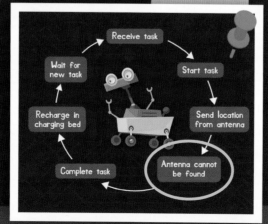

Receive task

Wait for new task

Start task

Recharge in charging bed

Send location from antenna

Complete task

Antenna cannot be found

### PAGE 15
Use the clock's hour hand, which is the smaller one, to count back six numbers from 2 p.m. The time will be 8 a.m.

### PAGE 19
The dog's fur matches the color of the fur found on the antenna.